Original title:
Words Under the Willow

Copyright © 2025 Creative Arts Management OÜ
All rights reserved.

Author: Julian Carmichael
ISBN HARDBACK: 978-1-80567-374-3
ISBN PAPERBACK: 978-1-80567-673-7

Eloquent Whispers in the Dusk

In the shade where secrets bend,
A squirrel spills the gossip trend.
He chatters loud, with no distress,
While all the leaves plot their finesse.

Beneath the boughs, the shadows play,
A raccoon juggles, hip hooray!
The breeze joins in with a playful shush,
As echoes dance in a silly hush.

A frog croaks jokes, with glee it sings,
About the shoes that cats can bring.
The fireflies titter, lighting up the night,
In this quirky realm, we're filled with delight.

With laughter spilling at dusk's embrace,
Every critter wears a smiling face.
So gather round, let stories unfold,
In the twilight where mischief is bold.

Shadows Speak in Silence

A shadow danced on my big toe,
With a laugh that made the grass grow.
It whispered secrets of the night,
While I just chuckled at its fright.

The moon peeked out, a cheeky grin,
As shadows played like children in.
They told of frogs with fancy hats,
And mice who learned to do acrobats.

The starlight giggled in the trees,
As breezes tickled under leaves.
I couldn't help but join the cheer,
For shadows spoke, and I could hear.

With every tale, I felt more wise,
As brightness sparkled in their eyes.
Who knew that silliness could gleam,
In silent shadows, we can dream!

Ink of the Forest Floor

The forest floor was quite the find,
With ink spills made by squirrel kind.
Each nut, a pen, each twig a line,
Amusing tales from trees divine.

A rabbit wrote about his stew,
While hedgehogs penned a jungle zoo.
The grass sang songs of summer cheer,
Where ink spilled laughter, oh so dear.

A tiny ant became the bard,
Reciting poems in the yard.
Each critter giggled at the rhyme,
In a fancy manuscript of thyme.

So come and join this leafy plot,
Where words are wild and laughter's hot.
The forest whispers tales so bright,
In every laugh, a spark of light!

Leafy Tales Unraveled

A leaf fell down to share a joke,
About a tree that tried to poke.
It missed the cloud, but hit the ground,
And giggles echoed all around.

The sunbeam joined with laughter bright,
As petals spun in pure delight.
Each story told, a spark of fun,
With every beam, the joy begun.

A nutcase squirrel wrote the script,
With acorn caps and laughter tipped.
While nature scribbled in the breeze,
Creating tales that danced with ease.

So gather 'round this leafy stage,
And let your heart be light, not sage.
For in the rustle and the play,
Leafy tales chase the gloom away!

Phrases Carved by Time

In bark of trees, old phrases dwell,
Of squirrels frolicking—oh, so well.
They say the winds have tales to tell,
Of silly deeds and rings of shell.

The owls hooted in delight,
At phrases etched in soft moonlight.
Each curve and swoop, a wondrous sight,
In woven tales that took their flight.

And mushrooms giggled underground,
With every phrase—a merry sound.
They whispered secrets 'neath the ground,
In every laugh, a joy profound.

So listen close, dear friend of mine,
For time has carved a witty line.
In every tale, a twisty chime,
That echoes long, beyond our time!

Breaths of the Enchanted

A squirrel dropped an acorn, just missed my hat,
It rolled by my foot, oh, how silly was that!
The bird in the branches laughed with delight,
As I danced like a fool, trying to take flight.

The tree swayed and giggled, a whimsical sound,
While I spun in circles, feet barely off ground.
It chuckled in whispers, a breeze in my ear,
Telling tales of mischief that brought me good cheer.

Secrets Beneath the Bough

A rabbit in spectacles read me a book,
He paused for a second, with one funny look.
"These tales of adventure are quite the affair,
But why wear a bowtie if you've got no flair?"

I promised to dress him in polka dot shoes,
He winked and declared he'd join me in blues.
With each rustle of leaves, laughter echoed bright,
As we plotted our outfits to dazzle the night.

Rhyme and Reason in the Stillness

A turtle once claimed he could jog to the moon,
With a wink and a nod, oh, what a buffoon!
I chuckled and asked, "But how do you fly?"
He shrugged, spinning tales of a turtle's sky-high.

Underneath all the branches, shadows danced true,
While frogs sang their croaking, a comical tune.
We pondered if lemons could grow on a vine,
"Or maybe just jellybeans? Wouldn't that be fine?"

Metaphors Draped in Nature

The butterflies whispered between petals bright,
"Your hair is a mess, but it's a glorious sight!"
I opened my eyes to their colorful flight,
And chuckled at ants in their serious plight.

A snail slipped and tripped on a leaf with a thunk,
While I tried to contain all my rollicking funk.
Nature's a stage for the silliest plays,
As laughter erupts through the sun's gentle rays.

Beneath the Weight of Leaves

Squirrels conspire, with acorns to hide,
Dancing in circles, with no place to bide.
An owl plays chess, with a wise old crow,
Each piece made of twigs, a feathered show.

The sun yawns loud, while grasshoppers sing,
In shades of green, they claim it's spring.
A leaf hits the ground, what a splendid flop,
And down comes a raindrop, with a splat and a pop.

Echoes of Nature's Heart

A frog in a tie, recites Shakespeare's verse,
While ants take bets, on who'll win the curse.
A melody hums, from the bugs' tiny band,
With drumsticks of twigs, they play quite unplanned.

The breeze tells a joke, but it flutters away,
Grass whispering secrets, they dance and they sway.
A bumblebee sneezes, causing a fumble,
As the flowers all giggle, their petals all tumble.

Starlit Confessions on the Lawn

The moon, feeling bold, spills secrets of night,
Cats on the prowl, with glimmers of fright.
A couple of fireflies, in love's tango bright,
Twinkling like crazy, in soft, glowing light.

While crickets complain, about lack of a tune,
As raccoons sneak off, with bright silver spoons.
The wind starts to chuckle, it's up to some tricks,
As the shadows all leer, plotting mischief and kicks.

Footnotes Beneath the Sky

Under the boughs, we scribble our tales,
Of mischief and snacks, of stealthy snails.
A caterpillar wears, a curious hat,
As butterflies argue, just where is the mat?

A picnic gone wrong, with ants in a line,
Claiming our crumbs like they were divine.
The sun sets in laughter, the day hugs the night,
While whispers of wonder, dance out of sight.

Serenade of the Swaying Limbs

The branches dance, they tease the breeze,
Whispers of laughter rustle through leaves.
A squirrel dons a tiny top hat,
As down below, the mushrooms chat.

The bumblebees wear polka dots bold,
While the ants tell tales of treasures untold.
The breeze carries giggles, such a delight,
Even the shadows join in the spite.

A thrush starts to croon a silly tune,
As crickets tap dance, oh what a boon!
The late sun paints everything gold,
In this woodland, tales of joy unfold.

Chronicles of the Quiet Grove

In the quiet grove where secrets bubble,
Rabbits gossip and create a hubble.
The willows wear a leafy crown,
And spider squirrels wear tiny frowns.

Frogs compete in a singing spree,
Croaking verses with utmost glee.
A quiet tree holds a secret show,
As fireflies put on a light-filled glow.

A snail just claimed the title of fast,
While bees mockingly cheer, 'You'll never last!'
Underneath the old oak, frogs leap and bound,
In this foolishness, pure joy is found.

Spells Cast in Green Hues

A witch with a broom as crooked as can be,
Mixes potions in a gnarled tea tree.
Her cat plays tricks, juggling with bones,
While snickering owls share silly groans.

Toadstools form a ring of bright red,
While tiny pixies dance on their heads.
'Curse you, you rogue!' one tiny sprite shouts,
But giggles and grins are what it's about.

An old gnome snorts as he sips his brew,
Hiccups a rainbow, much to the dew.
The air is alive with magical fun,
Casting spells till the day is done.

Reflections at Twilight's Edge

At twilight's edge, the shadows play,
Frogs in tuxedos leap ballet.
Fireflies flicker, a sparkling sight,
Dancing around in the fading light.

Laughter echoes from a chipmunk clan,
Who chuckle with jest at the passing man.
A tap-dancing raccoon steals every glance,
And even the grass seems to prance.

Under the whispering tree's embrace,
A breeze carries secrets from place to place.
The day bows out to the moon's white tease,
In this magical moment, we giggle with ease.

The Language of Shaded Vistas

In the shade where squirrels play,
Chasing dreams on a sunny day.
Each giggle echoes, a playful leap,
While the world around them, secrets keep.

A bee buzzes by, with a wink and a grin,
As ants form lines, marching in sin.
They bring their own flair, oh what a sight!
In this shady arena, everything's light.

The grass talks back with a rustling cheer,
While daisies gossip, lending an ear.
The breeze tosses tales, and all join the fun,
Under the leaves, laughter's never done.

So let's dance with shadows, as day turns to night,
In this world of whimsy, where joy takes flight.
With every step, a new jest unfolds,
In the language of laughter that nature holds.

Reverberations Among the Roots

Beneath the surface, the roots do chat,
Sharing rumors of a sly little bat.
"To the moon!" one shouted, "Let's fly high!"
While leaves above rolled their eyes with a sigh.

A turtle wanders, slow but so wise,
Offering tales of the clouds in disguise.
"Have you seen," he asks with a nod so sly,
"Those raindrops fall, like fish from the sky?"

The mushrooms giggle, their caps all a-twist,
As shadows throw shade on the daylight kissed.
"Oh dear," they say, "What a silly lot!
We're all just roots trying to see what's hot!"

With echoes of laughter in earthy delight,
They chortle through days and frolic by night.
In this secret realm, where the gentle hums,
The reverberations of joy find their drums.

Tides of Time Beneath the Canopy

In the twilight's glow, the beetles parade,
Their tiny legs tapping, a grand charade.
"Oh look," one shouts, "watch me dance!"
While fireflies twinkle, enhancing the chance.

The branches lean in, exchanging some views,
A debate on which color is better in hues.
"Orange is superb!" said a thrilled little bud,
While another exclaimed, "But blue's what I'd thud!"

As the moon peeks down, a wink on her face,
The shadows do jiggle, keeping up pace.
"Who's got the time?" asks the wise old owl,
"Let's revel in moments, we'll never scowl!"

Under the stars, tales ripple and twist,
In these sweet currents, no joy is missed.
For in the tides that flow through the night,
The laughter of creatures creates pure delight.

Whirling Words in the Whispering Breeze

With every gust, the trees start to chuckle,
As petals take flight and begin to chuckle.
"I'll soar to the top!" a brave little leaf,
While the others just giggle, sparking belief.

The breeze skips by, a jester in green,
Whispering jokes, oh have you seen?
A dandelion's wish is caught in the air,
"I'll wish for more wishes!" it said with a flair.

Butterflies flutter, with laughter they swoop,
"Catch me if you can!" they challenge the group.
And the flowers below wear their brightest of grins,
As they cheer for the daredevils, flaunting their spins.

Under the canvas of skies so grand,
The whirling of whispers takes a brave stand.
And in this revival, where giggles are free,
Words playfully swirl, like leaves on the spree.

Whispers Beneath the Canopy

Beneath the branches, jokes collide,
Squirrels chuckle, their tails in pride.
Rabbits gossip while munching on grass,
Even the ants are part of the class.

Leaves flutter down, like notes from a friend,
With every rustle, the laughter won't end.
A beetle in shades now offers snark,
While shadows stretch long in the park.

The sun sneezes, and everyone jumps,
A dance of confusion, a bundle of clumps.
Branches shake loose their leafy attire,
And butterflies giggle around the fire.

So gather beneath this leafy delight,
Where humor and nature unite in their flight.
In this jovial grove, smiles abound,
As giggles and whispers float all around.

Secrets in the Shade

In the cools of the noon, secrets do twirl,
As socks on a dog start to unfurl.
Trees trade tales of mischief and fun,
While critters convene, their work never done.

A snail slips by with a grin so wide,
Claiming he raced, but he's got no pride.
The frogs croak puns about flies and bugs,
While the grass hums softly, full of warm hugs.

Under the shade where the shadows can play,
Lies a treasure of laughter that brightens the day.
As fireflies blink like mischievous spies,
The whispers of secrets lend joy to our sighs.

So stay for a while in this playful glade,
Where mischief is bubbly, and pranks are well-made.
Here laughter dances, and silence takes flight,
In the heart of the shade, what a marvelous sight!

Echoes of Silken Leaves

Soft leaves chatter in a breeze so light,
Sharing the tales of a curious night.
A raccoon's mask twinkles with flair,
As he recounts stories of a midnight scare.

Sunlight drips honey on everything near,
While the woodpecker taps like he's drumming a cheer.
Grasshoppers leap while the bugs kick their feet,
In this glossy amphitheater, life is a treat.

A butterfly winks, with glittering glee,
Telling the ants about fancy tea.
The brooks splash laughter, a bubbly refrain,
As daisies giggle, their heads held in vain.

Amidst this chatter where lunacy thrives,
Nature's own circus, where humor derives.
So linger a while, let laughter unfold,
In the echoes of leaves, pure joy to behold!

Letters Lost in the Breeze

A paper plane sails through the air with ease,
Drifting away on a whim of the breeze.
It spills its secrets to forgetful trees,
As tittering whispers float past the bees.

The font of the tale is quite misunderstood,
As shadows eavesdrop, seen as they're good.
A clumsy squirrel trips on a nut so round,
Falling head over feet on the soft ground.

A lizard grins, plotting his next spree,
While a chipmunk dons a hat for a fee.
Leaves shimmy and shake, a wild charmeuse,
In a ballet of breezes, partake of the muse.

So come join the chatter, let laughter soar,
In this land of whimsy, where joy's at the core.
As letters get lost, new stories begin,
Where fun fills the air, let the game spin!

Lullabies of the Leafy Canopy

In a tree where squirrels play,
I heard a crow rant just today.
He said, 'This branch is mine, you see!'
While munching nuts quite glibly free.

The breeze whispered tales so wild,
Of raccoons who dance like a child.
They trip and tumble, what a sight!
Under the stars, they laugh at night.

A woodpecker knocked like a DJ,
Announcing parties the fun way.
But when a rabbit stole the show,
He made a DJ's hat from snow!

In the shade where shadows dart,
Each critter plays a funny part.
With giggles shared and laughter loud,
The canopy's a playful crowd.

Soliloquies of the Sylvan Grove

A fox stood still, his nose in the air,
'Why do trees grow with such flair?'
He pondered deeply, lost in thought,
While ants just marched, 'Hey, we're not caught!'

A turtle sighed, 'Oh, what a pace!
Everything here is in a race!'
But as he climbed a mossy hill,
He took a nap, and time stood still.

A chipmunk claimed, 'I own this glade,'
While stealing seeds from all that laid.
His friends just rolled their tiny eyes,
And joined him in a game of spies.

From lofty branches, laughter flew,
Each creature danced, as if they knew.
In playful banter, life's a jest,
The sylvan grove is simply the best!

Murmurs Among the Roots

Beneath the bark, the gossip flows,
Of tree friends talking in hushed lows.
'He thought he'd grow a little tall!'
'But roots said nope, he's got no balls!'

A worm chimed in, 'I heard a tale,
Of a branch that tried to go sail!'
They laughed and rolled in dirt so fine,
'With no sails! Oh, what a line!'

A dreamer fern whispered with glee,
'Why not root for a leafy spree?'
And as the laughter shook the ground,
The joyful chatter danced around.

Each secret shared, a bond took flight,
Among the roots where jesters bite.
In nature's jest, they find their youth,
In every giggle, there's a truth.

Verses in the Verdant Veil

When sunlight dapples through the leaves,
The forest hums, and laughter weaves.
A frog recites a haiku loud,
While fish in ponds cheer him proud.

A hedgehog wore a tiny hat,
And danced around, oh, fancy that!
The butterflies clapped their wings,
Enchanted by such silly flings.

A breeze blew through a willow fine,
'No smoking here, I've drawn the line!'
The trees all shook, their branches swayed,
And underfoot, the fairies played.

In verdant realms, absurdity reigns,
With giggles sprouting like small grains.
Each murmur shared in laughter's hold,
A tapestry of joy retold.

Songs of the Sighing Boughs

Beneath the branches, whispers play,
Squirrels debating, who's on the tray.
Laughter echoes, as bees take flight,
Nature's joke, what a funny sight!

A crow mocks a cat, what a scene,
Dancing shadows, all bright and green.
The wind tells tales, silly and grand,
Tickling the leaves, who understand!

Roots gossip softly, secrets they share,
As rabbits hop about without a care.
Every twig bends, with a chuckle or two,
In the realm of laughter, all creatures accrue!

While shadows wink at the light of day,
Even the sunlight begins to sway.
In this leafy stage, all is surreal,
Join in the laughter, it's a hearty meal!

Melodies of the Gentle Earth

Crickets compose symphonies at night,
A frog croaks the bass, to everyone's delight.
Daisies giggle in a breeze so light,
As fireflies dance in a flashing flight.

The earth spins jokes, round and round,
While mushrooms laugh, oh, what a sound!
Ants march in tune, with tiny boots,
With a conductor, a snail in pursuit!

Leaves unfold stories from far and wide,
Of lazy clouds and a starry ride.
Underfoot, the soil hums along,
A funny little ditty, nature's song!

Twirling petals, like dancers on cue,
Swirling laughter, in morning's dew.
Each note a giggle, each breeze a snort,
In this gentle realm, we all cavort!

Voices Drifting through the Leaves

From the treetops, whispers float and fly,
A raccoon complains, 'Did you see that guy?'
Swaying branches share secrets with glee,
Nature's gossip, just wait and see!

Larks sing out, with a cheeky refrain,
As frogs join in, like a wild campaign.
The wind carries tales of missed opportunities,
Of funny blunders and odd little communities!

With a rustle here, and a flap of a wing,
Shake your head at the nonsense they bring.
Leaves chuckle softly, in rustling fits,
While squirrels debate, who's the best at tricks!

Every creak is a punchline well-timed,
In this leafy playground, laughter's prime!
So join the fun, in this arboreal spree,
Where voices drift freely, happy and free!

The Essence of Stillness

In the quiet nooks, a stillness prevails,
Yet giggles abound, like tiny gales.
A pebble ponders, as ants march past,
'What's the rush? Life's fleeting, make it a blast!'

A ladybug winks, sharing inside jokes,
While turtles chuckle, as wisdom invokes.
The calm might deceive, but oh, look close,
Every hush is filled with laughter, a dose!

Breezes whisper softly, in gentle tones,
While shadows dance lightly over stones.
A tale unfolds with each rustle and pause,
As even the quiet unveils its applause!

So here's to the stillness, a teasing hush,
Where every moment has its merry rush.
In the essence of calm, let giggles arise,
In this serene laughter, nature's sweet surprise!

Epiphanies in Enchanted Groves

In the grove where shadows play,
A squirrel starts to dance all day.
He flips and twirls, oh what a sight,
Chasing butterflies in sheer delight.

A rabbit joins with a funny laugh,
While ants parade like a comic staff.
The trees nod gently, sharing a jest,
As laughter echoes, nature's guest.

In whispers soft, the leaves proclaim,
That life is best when it's a game.
So grab a seat on this grassy mound,
Let silly faces and giggles abound.

As twilight falls, the crickets sing,
Of quirky tales, and joyous things.
In this enchanted space, we find,
A world of whimsy, so sweetly kind.

Imagined Stories in the Shade

Beneath the tree, a tale is spun,
Of pirates, mermaids, oh what fun!
A turtle in a captain's coat,
Swabs the deck of a floating boat.

The parrot squawks, with flair and sass,
A villain lurking in tall grass.
Yet every plot takes a twist or turn,
As laughter echoes, the branches yearn.

A picnic basket, filled with dreams,
Of sandwiches and giggling schemes.
We munch and laugh, our spirits fly,
In this shady nook, we never sigh.

And as we weave our silly lore,
Old trees giggle, wanting more.
The sun drifts low, our stories grow,
In this fun-filled shade, we'll overflow.

Syllables Swaying with the Breeze

The breeze dances, with whispers light,
Carrying syllables, playful and bright.
A juggler stumbles, balls in the air,
As nearby flowers giggle without a care.

Rabbits debate on who hops best,
While a turtle claims he's quite the jest.
The wind chuckles at their little squabble,
With every gust, it's all just gobble.

In this playground of nature's cheer,
Each sound a note, each smile sincere.
As daisies sway to an unseen beat,
We laugh and clap, our joy complete.

So here we sit, hearts in full bloom,
In this lighthearted, breezy room.
Nature's chorus, so wild and free,
Where silliness flows, like the sea.

Prose in the Peaceful Retreat

In a corner where the silence beams,
Prose takes flight, escaping dreams.
A dog with glasses reads aloud,
As birds gather, forming a crowd.

The cat ponders on the meaning of life,
While squirrels plot to avoid the strife.
With every word that mixes and swirls,
Laughter bubbles as imagination unfurls.

Beneath the branches, ideas ignite,
With charming puns and laughter bright.
Each line a giggle, each sentence a glee,
We sip on joy, oh how carefree!

So here in this retreat, we find our muse,
In prose so funny, we never lose.
With echoes of humor in every seat,
We dance through the pages on whimsy's beat.

Elegies Whispered at Dusk

Beneath the branches, shadows dance,
Squirrels debate their chance of romance.
A frog tells tales of grand exclamations,
While crickets play tunes for the astonished creations.

A raccoon recites in exaggerated tones,
As fireflies gossip in flickering tones.
The owl hoots laughter, playful and bold,
While daisies gossip, sharing secrets untold.

Laughter erupts, a party of jest,
As bugs wear their hats, they're looking their best.
They dance in a circle, a furry delight,
In twilight's embrace, fading into the night.

As we tiptoe away, slipping from sight,
The willow chuckles, secrets held tight.
In leafy repose, it guards the absurd,
A symphony of joy, conveyed without word.

Chronicles of the Rustling Leaves

Leaves giggle secrets in the breeze's warm hug,
A squirrel dons glasses to read from a mug.
The winds play pranks, giving branches a shake,
While rabbits hold meetings, planning their break.

A crow caws riddles, not one is profound,
While grasshoppers jump up and down on the ground.
As summer's sun tickles the treetop's high crown,
The forest erupts; there's nothing to frown.

Beneath bright acorns, a gathering sprawls,
Where ants play charades and the laughter just sprawls.
The ladybugs vote on the best little dance,
While beetles compete in a chance at romance.

The evening grows dim, twinkling stars peek,
The leafy assembly grows tired but chic.
With one last hurrah, they bow to the night,
The chronicles written, in leaves taking flight.

Harmonies of the Hallowed Ground

Beneath the old oak, the frogs sing a tune,
A melody mixed with the light of the moon.
The grass hums softly, swaying with cheer,
While fireflies dance, mischief holds dear.

A hedgehog complains of the lack of a band,
As turtles tap tempo with feet in the sand.
An orchestra forms, though quite hard to align,
With sporadic applause from the insects divine.

A woodpecker joins in, with a drum on the bark,
As shadows regroup to perform in the dark.
The crickets are soloists taking their stage,
In laughter and music, they're all quite engaged.

The concert concludes with a grand, merry bow,
As night wraps the woods in its velvety vow.
While stars join the dance, in a wink and a spin,
The harmonies linger, embodying win.

Thoughts Woven in Green

In a patch of soft clover, a rabbit declares,
"I only wear socks when I'm caught unawares!"
The daisies chuckle, they know what he means,
While ladybugs giggle at cotton-filled seams.

A chatter of breezes, the sun sinks low,
A tale of a snail, and its worries to grow.
With each pass of a leaf, new gossip is spun,
As whimsical whispers turn work into fun.

A wobbly worm recites poems in pies,
While puppies roll 'round, catching beams from the skies.

The ants march in patterns, a synchronized march,
While neighboring toads hold their own little arch.

As darkness creeps in, the stories don't cease,
In the heart of green, we find laughter's fleece.
With each dappled moment, good nature prevails,
In thoughts woven lightly, where humor unveils.

A Symphony of Silent Thoughts

The bird sang a tune, quite absurd,
While squirrels danced, quite unconcurred.
Leaves swayed gently, no one could tell,
What secrets they held, under their shell.

A frog leapt high, with a comedic flair,
Land ed right there, without a care.
The breeze had a giggle, the grass waved back,
In this melody of nature, nothing's off track.

Even the sun chuckled, warm on my face,
As shadows played games, a delightful chase.
With every rustle, laughter ensued,
In this symphony, happiness brewed.

So here I sit, with thoughts in mine,
Nature's humor, a glorious sign.
In every chirp and ripple's spree,
A funny world, wild and free.

Nature's Annotations Beneath the Sky

Dandelions doodle on the grassy page,
While butterflies flutter, wise for their age.
A snail writes slowly, a story quite grand,
Of epic adventures in a tiny land.

Clouds scribble notes in a whimsical way,
Chasing the sunlight, not wanting to stay.
A breeze whispers jokes, just to amuse,
Nature's own laughter, for it can't lose.

Ants march in line, quite a busy parade,
Trading their secrets, in the shade they've made.
With every rustle, a punchline so sweet,
Life's little moments, can't be beat.

Underneath branches, where giggles can fly,
Nature's remarks float up to the sky.
With wit and with whimsy, the earth entertains,
Creating a gallery, in mud and in stains.

Ponderings Under the Playful Clouds

A rabbit with glasses reads the fine print,
While shadows chase sunbeams, in a sprint.
The clouds mock the shapes, as they drift by,
A seal, then a donut—oh my, oh my!

Kites dance above in a whimsical race,
Their tails wiggling wildly, in pure open space.
Trees nod their heads, gossiping low,
Sharing old tales only they know.

Sunflowers grin, while daisies chime in,
In this garden of laughter, all seek a win.
Butterflies crack jokes, quite absurd but bright,
Echoes of fun, in colorful flight.

So let's laugh with the breeze, sing with the sun,
In this meadow of cheer, there's always more fun.
With every soft giggle that floats on the air,
We'll ponder and chuckle, without any care.

Echoing Thoughts on the Riverbank

Pebbles skip tales, as the river flows,
With laughter that bubbles, and pure comic prose.
A fish with a hat flicks a wink my way,
In this playful world, who needs to sway?

Reflections chuckle at their own silly stance,
Playing tricks on the light, in a whimsical dance.
The trees whisper loudly, just like old friends,
Sharing their secrets, as laughter transcends.

Ducklings parade, all in a row,
Marching to music only they know.
With every soft ripple, joy does abound,
On this riverbank stage, fun's always found.

So let's dip our toes in this laughter-filled stream,
Where nature creates the most delightful dream.
With echoes of giggles that sing all around,
In this playful embrace, joy is unbound.

Fragments Found in Dusk's Embrace.

In twilight's glow, a squirrel pranced,
Chasing shadows, as if entranced.
His acorn stash, a game so grand,
Dropping treasures, a clumsy hand.

A chirp from above, a surprised finch,
Witnessing antics from a tree's pinch.
Giggles break free, wind joins the jest,
Nature's comedy, an unwritten fest.

A rabbit hops, tripping on root,
Spinning in circles, lost in pursuit.
The last of the light plays tricks on their spree,
As dusk wraps its arms 'round the wild jubilee.

Whispers Beneath the Ancient Tree

Beneath the branches, secrets do creep,
A ladybug snores, in slumber so deep.
Ants on parade, in a line so grand,
Marching like soldiers, across the green land.

A frog on a leaf, ready for fame,
Croaks a tune, though it isn't the same.
The wind starts to chuckle, rustles the leaves,
Can't help but giggle at nature's heaves.

A raccoon sneaks in, with a snack in tow,
Juggling berries, putting on a show.
With each little fumble, laughter erupts,
As tree trunks echo delight, it erupts.

Secrets in the Shade

In shady corners, mischief unfolds,
A mouse steals cheese, as the story is told.
The cat, oh so sly, lies low on the ground,
Plotting a pounce, though no prey is found.

A butterfly laughs, dancing carefree,
While ants roll a crumb, what a sight to see!
They trip on the dew, lose their grand haul,
Spinning in circles, yet proud, standing tall.

From high up a branch, an owl hoots with glee,
Winks at the clownfish swimming the sea.
It's chaos and joy, where creatures convene,
In the shade of the tree, life's silly routine.

Echoes of Swaying Branches

Above in the canopy, the branches sway,
As if they're grooving, come what may.
A breeze joins the party, rustling leaves,
Tickling the boughs, oh, what mischief it weaves!

A dog runs by, tail wagging with pride,
Dances through shadows, full of wild stride.
But trips on a twig, with a yelp of surprise,
Nature chuckles, oh, how time flies!

A pair of squirrels share tales of woe,
Fighting over acorns—quite the show!
As echoes of laughter drift through the park,
The woodland comes alive, bringing joy in the dark.

Sagas of Saplings and Shadows

Tiny trees in silliness sway,
Chasing shadows at the end of day.
Whispers giggle through the leaves,
As branches tell tales of mischief thieves.

Squirrels scamper in frantic glee,
While acorns plot their own jubilee.
The bark throws a party, come take a seat,
With roots that dance to the heartbeat's beat.

In the rustle, find playful spies,
With laughter carried in the skies.
The saplings strategize a plucky prank,
While sunlight bathes the shady bank.

Nature's antics, romps, and plays,
Compose the humor of their days.
With every breeze, a chuckle shared,
In this lively glen, all joy declared.

Reflections in the Tranquil Gloom

In the quiet, giggles rise,
As frogs wear crowns and sumo size.
With shadows stretching longer still,
The moon joins in with a quirky thrill.

Bats in capes take off in flight,
Pretending to be the stars at night.
A duck quacks like a bouncing ball,
While crickets chirp their night-time call.

The pond's surface becomes a show,
As fish perform underwater flow.
Reflections laugh in silver pools,
Where even the quietest hold their tools.

Gloom festoons in comedic guise,
With whispers that tickle and tantalize.
For here in mirth, shadows find grace,
In the tranquil gloom, a merry space.

Nurturing Narratives Within the Glade

In the glade where giggles sprout,
Laughter echoes, without a doubt.
Plants share secrets, not too wise,
In tales of clumsy bugs that fly.

Sunbeams dance like jesters bold,
While daisies gossip, stories told.
A caterpillar's fashion spree,
Leaves the others laughing free.

Every breeze hums a funny tune,
As trees shimmy under the moon.
Critters gather for the plot,
While shadows stretch in a silly knot.

Narratives twist beneath the sky,
Where even the grumpy trees can't deny.
In this glade, where fun is the theme,
Every leaf whispers a laughter dream.

Poetic Whispers of the Wilderness

Amidst the wild, whispers collide,
Echoing laughter, can't be denied.
With every rustle, a giggle takes flight,
As leaf and grass join the playful night.

Owls wear glasses, thinking they're wise,
While rabbits debate the best carrot size.
A turtle tells tales, so slowly they creep,
While snakes hang around in a cozy heap.

Nature pens gags, sketches absurd,
From prankster pine cones, never unheard.
Each twinkling star seems to bow with delight,
As foliage whispers secrets at night.

In this wilderness, humor roams free,
With playful creatures and plant jubilee.
So listen closely, lend an ear,
For poetic whispers of fun draw near.

Dialogues with the Dancing Shadows

The shadows giggle low and sly,
They whisper tales as time slips by.
A silhouette with a funny hat,
Says, "I just saw a dancing cat!"

The moon joins in, a cheeky grin,
"Let's take a spin, come on, let's spin!"
The stars start twinkling, oh so bright,
Waving to the shadows in the night.

"Why are you laughing?" asked a tree,
"Your silly steps are fun, you see!"
The shadows replied, "It's all in play,
We dance till dawn, then fade away."

So while the night bears witness true,
To shadows that prance without a clue.
Remember every giggle shared,
In the moonlight's secret, laughter's bared.

The Language of Leaves and Light

Leaves chatter softly in the breeze,
Exchanging gossip with such ease.
"Did you hear about the acorn's fall?
It landed near a dance hall!"

The sunlight chuckles, peeking through,
"Let's throw a party; I'll join you!"
A leaf replied, with a gleeful hop,
"I'll spin and twirl; I just can't stop!"

They flutter and sway, their laughter bright,
Celebrating joy in the fading light.
"If only the branches could hold a tune,
We'd have a concert 'neath the moon!"

But branches just creak with laughter divine,
As leaves do their dance, a sight so fine.
In a world where light and leaves collide,
Even nature knows how to enjoy the ride.

Enigmatic Echoes from Above

Up in the sky, a cloud took flight,
Said to the sun, "You shine so bright!"
The sun just laughed, "Oh, don't be coy,
I'm simply here to spread the joy!"

An echo chimed from distant hills,
"Who's throwing parties? It gives me thrills!"
"Not us," said the moon, "we just float here,
But shadows dance; oh, very near!"

Stars winked and twinkled in playful glee,
"Let's form a band, just you and me!"
But echoes replied, in a booming roar,
"Why not invite the clouds to explore?"

So they all joined in, a cosmic play,
Joking and jesting till the break of day.
With laughter that echoed through the endless night,
Nature's own secrets spun in delight.

Nature's Poetry in the Gentle Wind

The wind sings sweetly, a playful jest,
Tickling the flowers, it never rests.
"Hey there, daisies, why so shy?
Join the dance; let's reach the sky!"

The daisies giggled, swayed with grace,
"Only if you promise to pick up the pace!"
The wind swirled round, a cheerful twist,
Making a playlist, oh, so hard to resist!

"Let's write a poem with every breeze,
A rhyme for the bees, a tune for the trees."
Nature responded with rustling cheer,
As laughter echoed for all to hear.

So next time you feel a gentle nudge,
Remember it's nature, a playful judge.
With every gust, a tale spins anew,
In the rhythm of life, there's fun for you.

The Silent Song of the Ground

Beneath the green, the laughter stirs,
As squirrels dance and shake their furs.
A jester's crown made of acorns bright,
Tickles the roots with joy and light.

A worm with tales of secret quests,
Spins stories that put the ants to rest.
A beetle hums a tune so rare,
While grasshoppers gossip without a care.

The daisies sway, their heads in cheer,
While butterflies giggle, drawing near.
They whisper 'round the bark so stout,
In this earthy realm, it's laughter's route.

So let the sounds of nature play,
In this patch of green where fun holds sway.
For every rustle, there's humor found,
In the silent song of the merry ground.

Wisps of Wisdom Gently Spoken

In the shade, where shadows tease,
The breeze tells jokes with perfect ease.
A butterfly winks, a bee rolls its eyes,
While trees giggle under the sunny skies.

"Why did the oak go to the gym?"
To get its branches feeling trim!
The trees burst out in raucous cheer,
As each new pun drifts near and clear.

A squirrel claims he's the fastest of all,
While the tortoise grins, slow but tall.
The laughter echoes through the glade,
In a symphony where joy is made.

So gather round, with friends so dear,
For silly wisdom flows right here.
Each whispered joke, a tender token,
In the grove where love is unspoken.

Chronicles of Comfort in the Grove

In the arms of the trees, stories unfold,
Of mischief and antics, both brave and bold.
A woodpecker snaps its beak in glee,
As raccoons plan a late-night spree.

"Hear ye, hear ye, gather 'round!"
Said a wise old owl with a voice profound.
He shares tales of a squirrel who stole a shoe,
And gopher's escapades at the midnight dew.

Fragrant flowers nod, in on the jest,
As the sun dips low, they're feeling blessed.
A laughter-laden air fills the grove,
In cozy corners where friendship's strove.

So write your stories, let them flow,
In the chronicles of comfort, let love grow.
For every chuckle is a seedling sown,
In the hearts of all, this grove is home.

Fluid Thoughts Amidst Stillness

In quiet corners, the mind takes flight,
With fluid thoughts that dance in light.
A breeze tickles the leaves so shy,
As frogs croak tunes, under the sky.

"Why hop around?" a turtle mused,
"I'd rather stroll and not be bruised!"
While ducks quack quips from the pond's embrace,
And reeds sway gently, keeping pace.

Every shadow holds a chuckle tight,
In stillness, we find our fun and might.
The reflections play on water's face,
As ripples join in the laughter race.

So when the world gets busy and loud,
Seek the calm, embrace it proud.
For in the hush, hilarity's drilled,
In fluid thoughts, our joy is filled.

A Tapestry of Dappled Sun

The squirrel wore a tiny hat,
Sipping tea while on a mat,
He'd giggle softly to the bee,
Who buzzed in rhythm, wild and free.

The rabbits played a game of chess,
With acorns as their queens, no less,
They bounced around, both wise and spry,
As funny birds all flapped nearby.

A fox in boots, he strutted in,
With tales of daring, bound to win,
The leaves would chuckle, rustle cheer,
As sunlight danced and brought good cheer.

A tapestry spun with bright delight,
Where creatures banter day and night,
In dappled sun, they all unite,
To share their laughter, oh what a sight!

Soft Murmurs from the Ground

An ant in glasses read a book,
He paused to give the worm a look,
"What's a plot?" the worm inquired,
"I dig deep holes, I'm not inspired!"

The beetle danced a polka fine,
While crickets played a merry line,
The flowers swayed, all nodding heads,
As whispered secrets filled their beds.

A mouse in slippers twirled away,
With dreams of cheese and pastry play,
And on the ground, the fun did stir,
As laughter flowed like gentle purrs.

Soft murmurs crept through grass and clay,
Where tiny friends enjoy their day,
With cheeky jokes and joyful sound,
In nature's bosom, joy is found!

Fables of the Forest Floor

The owl wore spectacles so round,
He told a story, wise and profound,
A tale of cakes and pies so sweet,
That made the critters scurry and beat.

A hedgehog pranced with swagger bold,
In shoes of red, he broke the mold,
He sang of forests, fables grand,
While mushrooms tapped to his command.

The raccoon wore a dazzling tie,
While sharing snacks, oh my, oh my!
With every crunch, the trees would sway,
As laughter echoed, come what may.

In fables spun of joy and lore,
The forest floor was never bore,
Where once upon a giggle grew,
And every tale had something new!

The Language of Dappled Light

The sunbeams played a game of catch,
With leaves and shadows, what a batch!
A ticklish breeze would laugh and tease,
As squirrels scuttled with such ease.

In dappled light, a dance ensued,
The grasshoppers hummed, their spirits glued,
With every jump, they told a joke,
Even the trees began to poke.

The daisies chimed in with a shout,
While butterflies flitted all about,
Their colors twirled in joyous flight,
As nature sang in pure delight.

The language here was one of cheer,
Where laughter blossoms, oh so near,
In dappled light, all creatures spark,
A symphony that lights the dark!

Serenades of the Silver Bough

A silver bough sways with a grin,
Chasing squirrels that dart and spin.
The acorns fall like little bombs,
While birds chirp jokes in feathery psalms.

The sun peeks in, a mischievous glare,
Highlighting the leaves with a golden hair.
A raccoon plays tag with a drippy snail,
While laughter ensues like a silly tale.

Frog leaps high, a real comedian,
Catching flies like a magician's minion.
The owl rolls eyes, too wise for pranks,
Snoring softly, giving no thanks.

Oh, how the branches twist and sway,
As shadows dance in a cheerful display.
This merry place, where giggles grow,
Keeps secrets safe that only they know.

Chants of the Gentle Breeze

The breeze hums softly, a playful tease,
Tickling leaves, twirling with ease.
Dandelions burst in clouds of white,
Like puffed up pillows, a funny sight.

A ladybug struts in polka dot shoes,
While crickets tap out their jovial blues.
The daisies giggle, bowing low,
As the breeze continues its whimsical flow.

A butterfly flutters, a clown in flight,
Wobbling here, then darting out of sight.
The trees wear masks, like jesters at play,
In this carnival realm, come join the fray!

Each rustling leaf sings a light-hearted tune,
Under the watch of the mischievous moon.
Nature laughs, a merry brigade,
In the orchestra of shade where joy is made.

Reflections in the Dappled Light

In dappled light, shadows giggle bright,
Leaves share secrets in the warm daylight.
A chipmunk juggles acorns, oh so sly,
While the sun casts smirks that kiss the sky.

Tadpoles splash like they're in a race,
Chasing bubbles with a determined face.
The willows sway, gossiping trees,
Whispering tales like a warm summer breeze.

A squirrel drops its stash with a thud,
Landing right in a muddy puddle of mud.
Laughter erupts from the nearby brook,
As frogs croak gossip, how funny they look!

Reflective ripples dance on the stream,
Where nature paints joy in a vibrant theme.
All around, merriment grows,
In the dappled light where humor flows.

Stanzas of the Wind's Embrace

The wind twirls petals, a playful fling,
While leaves laugh loudly, joining in the swing.
A grasshopper sings with a croaky zest,
Bouncing so high, it's a funny jest.

A caterpillar dreams of wings it could wear,
But for now, it's just rolling with flair.
The fox trots by, with a curious glance,
Wondering why the flowers do dance.

In this realm of whimsy, hilarity reigns,
With whispers of breezes and comical gains.
The trees hold hands, swaying with glee,
In the wondrous waltz of nature's spree.

Oh, the giggles that echo in the tall grass,
As the wind whispers secrets as shadows pass.
Each rustle and flutter tells tales of delight,
In this whimsical world where joy takes flight.

Shadows of Silence

Beneath the leafy canopy,
A squirrel steals a pie,
While whispers of the breeze,
Swoon gently as they fly.

A frog croaks jokes to flies,
His audience is quite still,
Yet laughter echoes low,
Among the roots that thrill.

Chasing shadows, chasing dreams,
The grass tickles my toes,
A catnap in the hammock,
Where nobody really knows.

A raccoon builds a tower,
Out of shiny cans and spoons,
Who knew beneath the branches,
It'd be such a hoot of a tune?

Stories Woven with Roots

The old tree tells a tale,
Of branches bent with age,
As squirrels play poker cards,
In a woodsy, rave-like stage.

Each leaf has its own gossip,
Of bees that try to dance,
But end up in a tangle,
In pollen's sticky trance.

The shadows twist like stories,
In patterns made by sun,
Where every twist and turn,
Is a joker on the run.

Underneath the twisted roots,
Lies a treasure deep in jest,
A hoard of acorns whispering,
That nature knows best!

Echoes Among the Branches

High up in the branches,
The owls play hide and seek,
While tiny woodland critters,
Begin to squawk and squeak.

A lizard wears a sunhat,
As he suns upon a stone,
While a snail takes a selfie,
Making sure he's not alone.

The occasional giggle,
From a rabbit feeling bold,
Echoes through the foliage,
As stories are retold.

With shadows dancing lightly,
In a game of chase and play,
The branches hold their secrets,
As daylight slips away.

Lullabies of the Gentle Wind

Listen close and you will hear,
The grasshoppers hum a tune,
As ants wear tiny hats,
And dance beneath the moon.

Crickets chirp their rhythm,
In a symphony of night,
While fireflies flash their lanterns,
To add a twinkling light.

The breeze is like a storyteller,
With tales of mischief and fun,
As clouds drift like dreamers,
Beneath this glowing sun.

A lullaby from nature,
Sung softly to a tree,
Where every rustling leaf,
Is a note of harmony.

Lyrics from the Lying Leaves

Beneath the boughs, the leaves all cheer,
Telling tales that only squirrels hear.
A cat once danced, a dog stood still,
They laughed so hard, they rolled down the hill.

A frog in a top hat croaked a tune,
His clickety-clack made the daisies swoon.
While ants dressed up for their grand parade,
With tiny trumpets, their music serenade.

The ladybug twirled in circles of glee,
Singing of honey and flying trees.
The breeze chimed in with a giggle or two,
And soon all the grass blades were laughing too!

So listen close when the leaves all giggle,
They weave silly songs with a hearty wiggle.
In the shade of the tree, let your laughter ignite,
Where every whisper's a pure delight!

Refrains of the Rooted Whisper

Under the roots, a secret crew,
Composed of shadows and morning dew.
The mice hold meetings, the hedgehogs toast,
To echoes of laughter, that's what they boast!

A raccoon in glasses read a book,
He wore a bow tie and had quite the look.
"Let's start a band!" he enthusiastically declared,
But the porcupine said, "I'm too spiked to be shared!"

A worm with a mustache played the guitar,
While ants tap danced under a shining star.
Each twirl and twang made the grass blades sway,
And all the critters sang night into day.

So if you should wander and hear a jest,
Remember beneath, where they strive for the best.
The whispers beneath, they giggle with glee,
In the heart of the roots, camaraderie!

Fairy Tales in the Forest's Heart

In the forest's heart, where giggles abound,
Lived a fox with a hat, quite renowned.
He told the best tales with a wink and a grin,
While deer clapped their hooves, encouraging him!

An owl in a cloak ran a drama club show,
The rabbits performed, stealing the glow.
Said the stage was a carrot, oh what a sight!
With each act, they bounced under the moonlight!

A bear with a flair led a dance on the hill,
While the frogs brought the beats with a rippling thrill.
They pranced and they twirled, no worries in sight,
Till the moon yawned wide and bid them goodnight!

So when twilight drapes its deep velvet hue,
Listen for laughter from each leafy cue.
For in this tale, joy is the thread,
With dreams woven softly on hearts that are fed!

Untold Stories Beneath the Canopy

Beneath the canopy, where mischief abounds,
A mischievous chipmunk pranced round and round.
With acorns as props, he put on a show,
While the bunnies threw popcorn from rows in a row!

A firefly director lit up the scene,
With glimmers of gold, and a sparkle of green.
The skunk played the lead, a surprise in the script,
And they laughed as a berry pie bobbled, then tipped!

The tree trunk became a great roaring stage,
With laughter and antics that lit up each page.
As squirrels shouted lines in their nutty little way,
The songs flowed like rivers; it brightened the day!

So stroll through the shade where joy's never shy,
Beneath the green boughs, let your worries fly.
For every giggle and chuckle you see,
Are untold stories made just to be free!

Musings in Nature's Embrace

A squirrel with a nut in tow,
He thinks he's quite the show.
The trees laugh at his fumble,
Nature's dance, a happy jumble.

A butterfly in a fluttery race,
Chasing shadows, a silly chase.
It lands on a leaf, then slips away,
Who knew nature could be so play?

Birds chirp jokes in melodic tones,
While rabbits hop on their little phones.
Every critter joins in the cheer,
Making the woods their comedy sphere.

Beneath the trees in splendid view,
Life feels like an ongoing review.
In this quirky, lively space,
We embrace nature's funny grace.

Reverie in the Rustic Grove

In the glade, a frog sings bright,
Claiming he's the king tonight.
A rabbit argues, "What a joke!
You can't rule with a voice that croaks!"

Leaves gossip about the sun,
"Why is he always on the run?"
Clouds giggle, sharing the tease,
As they float upon the breeze.

A turtle claims he's fast as light,
While the snail just rolls in delight.
"Patience is my secret art,"
He winks with a clever heart.

Fun lingers in the shade so wise,
Nature paints with bright surprise.
In laughter, every creature revels,
As life's humor softly levels.

Tales Carried by the Stream

The babbling brook tells silly tales,
Of fish who wear tiny scales.
A minnow struts like he's the best,
While a turtle snoozes, quite at rest.

Ducks quack about their mallard style,
Flipping feathers with great guile.
"Do you think we could fly?" one sighs,
"Only if clouds drop and rise!"

A beaver works with fortitude,
Building homes with a funny mood.
Chasing sticks, chaos ensues,
Splashing about in playful hues.

Onward flows the stream with glee,
Where laughter echoes, wild and free.
Nature, rich with jokes and cheer,
Fills our hearts with love sincere.

Dreams Cradled in Soft Light

Stars twinkle like a glittering crew,
"Did you see that? Did you?" they coo.
The moon rolls over with a grin,
"Hey, let's see who's next to win!"

Fireflies blink in a dance divine,
Flashing secrets, forming a line.
"Catch me if you can!" they tease,
Like tiny, glowing, mischief-y bees.

The night whispers jokes on the breeze,
As crickets chirp with rhythmic ease.
A raccoon steals a midnight snack,
With a cheeky grin, he'll not look back.

In the twilight's soft embrace,
Joyful rambles, a humorous chase.
For in the dreams that take their flight,
Laughter shines through the soft light.

Intimate Monologues of Nature

A squirrel once thought he could sing,
But all that came out was a fling.
He hopped with glee on a mossy stone,
While birds just rolled eyes, showing their tone.

A bee tried to dance, slipped on a leaf,
Buzzing loud, causing much grief.
The ants lined up, just to complain,
About how he dares not to remain.

The brook babbled secrets, oh what a mess,
Raccoons looked on, they couldn't care less.
The frogs joined in, wearing their best,
Croaking loudly, putting talents to test.

The great old oak, wise and stout,
Chuckled at all the ruckus about.
"Let them be funny, let them be wild,
Nature, my dear, is forever beguiled."

Reflections of Rustling Serenity

The breeze whispered jokes to the daffodils,
Making them giggle with all their thrills.
They swayed in rhythm, showing off grace,
While the tulips blushed, holding their place.

A turtle in slow-mo, took a grand stroll,
Looking for snacks, or maybe a roll.
He met a butterfly, quite full of cheer,
"Are you just stuck, or is this the frontier?"

The hedgehogs proposed a grand conga line,
But stumbled and tumbled, oh how divine!
The blossoms all laughed, petals in a twist,
As it formed a scene that would surely persist.

The grasshoppers danced, legs all amiss,
Join us, they shouted, come share in bliss!
With giggles and rustles, the garden agreed,
For light-hearted laughter is all they do need.

Timeless Tales in the Twilight

Under a blanket of shimmering light,
The fireflies gathered, oh what a sight!
They shared tales of old, of the moon's big hat,
And how it once fell on a lady cat.

The crickets, with violins, played a sweet tune,
As owls exchanged glances, looking at the moon.
"Who's there?" asked one with a sly old grin,
"Is that you, shadow, or just a twin?"

A fox recounted how he danced with the night,
But tripped on a root, what a silly fright!
His friends couldn't help but fall in a heap,
As laughter rang out while the shadows creep.

With giggles still echoing in twilight's embrace,
The tales of mischief painted each face.
For though time may halt, and darkness may fall,
The funny moments are cherished by all.

Musings Under the Lacy Branches

A caterpillar with dreams of a flight,
Scribbled on leaves, by the pale moonlight.
Said, "One day I'll flutter! Just wait and see,"
While a wise spider shrugged, sipping on tea.

The nightingale belted a brooding tune,
While the raccoons searched for snacks in the moon.
"Hey, those are mine!" one bird did squawk,
As the gang shuffled, plotting a midnight walk.

The shadows of flowers stretched far and wide,
As the ants boasted, "We never subside!"
But slipped on a dew drop, tumbled and rolled,
Creating a scene that was pure comedic gold.

And so under branches adorned with glee,
Nature laughed back, wild and free.
For who knew the night held such charming plays,
In laughter's embrace, all critters would stay.

Verses Found in the Woodland Whisper

In the forest, squirrels chatter loud,
While mushrooms giggle beneath a cloud.
Rabbits wear hats, tossing them high,
As dandelions dance, oh my, oh my!

A deer tells jokes with a wink and a nudge,
While crickets tap shoes, they won't even judge.
The wind shares secrets with the leaves so green,
As the sun pokes fun, bright and keen.

Beneath the pines, a fox takes a nap,
Dreaming of cheese, oh what a trap!
Songs of the birds, a comical tune,
Join in the laughter beneath the moon.

With a twiddle and a wobble, they sing,
As nature's orchestra plays its wild fling.
Laughter echoes through the tall oak trees,
In this woodland scene, joy's the breeze.

Interludes Beneath the Gnarled Trunks

Beneath old branches, owls make their plans,
With little squirrels plotting little scams.
A raccoon in spectacles reads a decree,
While turtles debate what fast really can be!

The groundhog provides the comic relief,
With punchlines that bring the trees disbelief.
While ants march around in a hilarious line,
Snapping their fingers to a rhythm divine.

A picnic basket rolls down the hill,
Squashed berries giggle, nature's wild thrill.
As bumblebees buzzing share their latest news,
About the flower party with funky new shoes.

In shadows of trunks, the humor grows,
As critters share tales that nobody knows.
With whispers and chuckles, they carry the night,
Under the gnarled trunks, everything feels right.

Hidden Messages of the Green Canopy

Up high in the leaves, where the whispers play,
A parrot tells secrets, come join the fray!
With each rustle and chuckle, the branches sway,
While the sunbeams giggle, lighting the way.

With acorns in hats, a party's in store,
As hedgehogs bring pastries, who could ask for more?
Frogs sketch their dreams in the mud, what a sight,
As fireflies twinkle, lighting up the night.

Conversations in vines wrap around tales,
Of snails racing turtles and their funny fails.
Mice on a mission, so bold and so brave,
Seeking treasures that only fools crave!

In this leafy world, where laughter's the theme,
Each creature's a player in nature's grand scheme.
With glee in the canopy, life's filled with fun,
As sunlight dances, the day's never done.

Harmonies of the Earthly Choir

The brook hums a tune with a jig and a jump,
While fish in the water perform quite the thump.
A family of ducks in a line sings along,
As frogs join the chorus in a ribbiting song.

With a shuffle and scamper, the critters all sway,
Creating a symphony through the bright day.
With crickets as drummers and bees as the beat,
The harmonies blend, oh what a treat!

Beetles wear tuxedos, prepared for a dance,
While ladybugs twirl in a vibrant romance.
Overhead, the larks craft a melodious cheer,
In the concert of nature, laughter is clear.

The harmony swells, filling the woodlands true,
As nature invites you to sing and to skew.
With every note lifted, every sound, a delight,
Within this grand choir, the world feels just right.

www.ingramcontent.com/pod-product-compliance
Lightning Source LLC
Chambersburg PA
CBHW071854160426
43209CB00003B/548